The Magic of A.C. Gilbert

by Robert Young
art by Mary Ann Nelson McAlister

Real Writing Press

Salem, Oregon

February 15, 1884

The day Alfred Carlton Gilbert was born, his parents could not have known the magic he would bring to the world. Nor could they have known the problems the boy would bring to them.

As a child, Alfred – called Gillie – whirled through the days racing tricycles, trapping squirrels, playing hooky, or planning a parachute jump off the roof of his house. Gillie did not rest for a moment.

Magic tricks kept Gillie's hands busy. From the day he earned his first magic kit, he loved doing tricks and practiced them hour after hour, day after day. "Step right up!" he'd say and his friends would gather around and watch as Gillie made coins disappear right before their eyes!

When Hermann the Great came to town, Gillie sat in the sold-out audience. His face lit up as the famous magician performed, and then his jaw dropped when Hermann invited him onto the stage. Gillie watched, spellbound, as Hermann pulled bananas, flowers, and even a rabbit out of the boy's pockets and sleeves!

Hermann finished with a flourish then turned to Gillie. "Don't you wish you could do things like this?" he asked.

"I can," answered Gillie, and reached for a deck of cards. He pulled a card from the deck, held it up for all to see, waved his hand and – PRESTO! - the card disappeared. As cheers filled the hall, Gillie took a bow.

When the Gilberts moved to Idaho, 8-year-old Gillie did not slow down to life in a small town. He worked long and hard hauling wood to heat the house, and still made time for fun: building a wild wagon ride, starting a guinea pig business, making his own fire department. And, of course, playing sports and performing magic too.

Gillie coaxed his two brothers to help him make a gymnasium in the barn so he could build up his small, slender body. He spent hours each day practicing his favorite activity, bag-punching. Soon, Gillie became an expert.

One day the manager from a traveling show came to the gym to watch him.

"Show me what you can do," the man said.

Gillie began hitting the bag – thap-thap-thap-thap-thap in perfect rhythm – first with his fists, then with his elbows, knees, head, and feet. Finally, he put on a blindfold and punched the bag without missing a beat.

"How old are you son?"

"Twelve."

"I've never seen anything like it!" the man exclaimed.

He immediately hired Gillie as the "Champion Boy Bag-Puncher of the World" at fifteen dollars a week. Gillie packed his bags and joined the show.

The job lasted less than a week, the time it took Gillie's father to find him and take him home.

Gillie's job ended, but not his life in sports. He kept practicing, and it paid off: world records for chin ups (40) and the running long dive (15' 9"). At Pacific University he quarterbacked the football team and captained the track team.

In 1905, Gillie moved across the country to Connecticut to study medicine at Yale. There he wrestled to a national championship and pole-vaulted to a world record (12' 7") and a gold medal at the 1908 Olympic games in London.

Practicing magic paid off in a different way. Now known as A.C., he performed at parties and clubs, earning up to $100 a night (equal to about $2,000 today).

A.C. also started a business making and selling boxed sets of magic tricks for $5 each. The money he earned helped him pay for college and support his new wife, Mary.

At last the day came when A.C. graduated from Yale. His parents traveled all the way from Oregon to attend the ceremony.

"We're so proud of you," his mother told him.

"You will make a fine doctor," said his father.

But A.C. had something else up his sleeve. He wanted to keep selling his boxes of tricks. He would be a businessman, not a doctor. A.C.'s parents were disappointed, but they knew their son had the magic to be a success in whatever he tried.

And they were right: A.C. sold many boxes of magic tricks. Still, he was not satisfied. A.C. wanted to expand into the toy business. All he needed was an idea.

The idea came in the fall of 1911 as A.C. rode the train home from New York City. He couldn't wait to share it that night with Mary.

"What is it, A.C.?" Mary asked when he rushed through the front door.

"We passed a construction site!" he gushed. "They had cranes lifting steel beams and making giant towers!"

Mary smiled, knowing that A.C. was up to something. Just like always.

"We can make toy construction kits!" he said. "Kids will love them!"

That night, A.C. and Mary cut cardboard into the shapes of small beams. The next day he took the cardboard pieces to a machinist, who made metal copies of them. Using nuts and bolts to connect the beams, A.C. made all sorts of models, everything from airplanes and bridges to Ferris wheels and windmills. He knew the construction kits would be a big hit.

A.C was right. Kids loved the kits, called Erector Sets. Thousands sold, making him a rich man.

Just when the future looked the brightest for the A.C. Gilbert Company, trouble came. The Great War – World War I. The United States tried to stay out of it, but in 1917 sent troops to Europe to fight Germany.

Christmas without toys? That would be like canceling the holiday! Toymakers boiled with anger. What would become of them if they couldn't sell toys? What would children do if they didn't have new toys to play with?

The toymakers had a meeting and made their own plan. They would send someone to Washington D.C. to talk to the council. They would send the man who had the magic to change the council's mind: A.C. Gilbert.

A.C. arrived in Washington, D.C. carrying some large packages. He would have only fifteen minutes of the council's time, but A.C. had an idea. He hoped it would work, for the sake of the toymakers and for kids everywhere.

When it was A.C.'s turn to speak, he looked across the room at the four powerful men who made up the council. It was the end of a busy day, and the men's faces were drawn tight, their shoulders slumped. A.C. knew he would have to choose his words carefully. They would be the most important words of his life.

"Toys are fun, but more than that," A.C said. "They start children on the road to construction, not destruction."

Slowly, the men's eyes lit with interest. A.C. went on, telling them toys help children learn and grow. Toys help children choose future jobs, and their work helps make America great!

Pausing, A.C. opened the packages. One by one he pulled out toys: a steam engine, tin soldiers, a magic kit, a submarine, an Erector Set. That's when the magic happened.

Men became boys again as they took the toys to the floor and played. As they played they talked.

"I learned about engineering playing with a steam engine."

"Where can I buy a submarine like this?"

"Toys appeal to the heart of every one of us, no matter how old we are."

Instead of fifteen minutes, the meeting stretched to three hours. Finally, the council gathered in a knot and spoke quietly. Then they announced their decision: toymakers could keep making toys. Christmas would not be canceled!

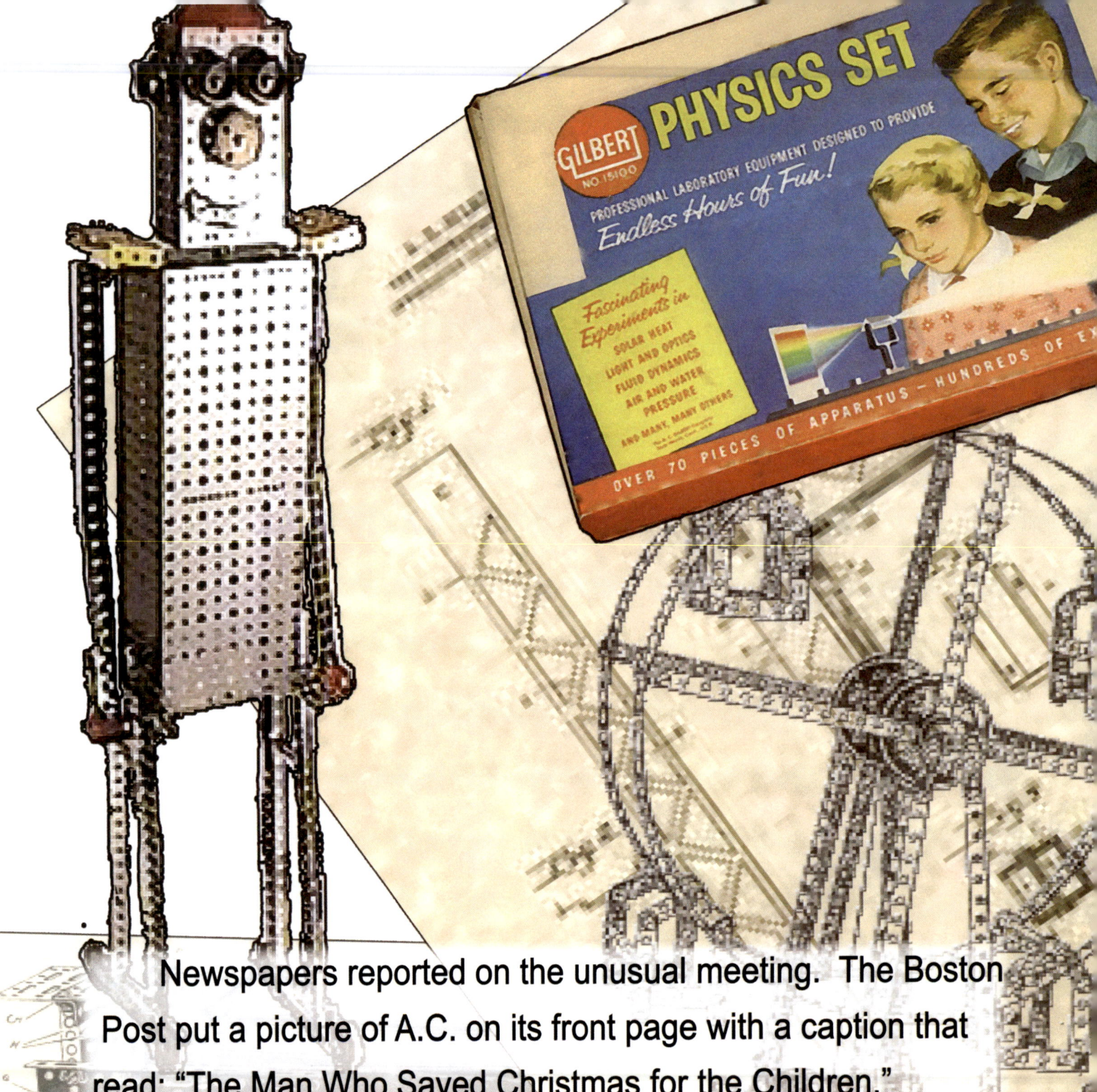

Newspapers reported on the unusual meeting. The Boston Post put a picture of A.C. on its front page with a caption that read: "The Man Who Saved Christmas for the Children."

After this, his greatest magic, A.C. still did not rest. He worked as hard as ever making toys that helped kids think and learn. New Erector Sets, science kits, and electric trains made the company a great success and A.C. Gilbert one of America's most famous toymakers.

A.C. Gilbert Timeline

1884 – Born in Salem, Oregon
1892 – Moves to Moscow, Idaho
1896 – Forms the Moscow Athletic Club in his barn
1901 – Sets the world record in chinups (40)
1902 – Enters Pacific University in Forest Grove, Oregon
        Sets the world record in the running long jump (15' 9")
1905 – Enters Yale University
        Wins the Intercollegiate Wrestling Championship
1908 – Wins the gold medal in pole-vaulting at the Olympic Games
        Marries Mary Thompson
1909 – Starts the Mysto Manufacturing Company
        Graduates from Yale University
1911 – Daughter Charlotte Gilbert is born
        Develops idea for Erector Sets
1913 – Introduces Erector Sets at the Toy Fair
1916 – Mysto Manufacturing Company becomes the A.C. Gilbert Company
1917 – Daughter Lucretia Gilbert is born
        Sells first chemistry sets
1918 – Persuades the National Defense Council not to cancel Christmas
1919 – Son Alfred Carlton Gilbert Jr. is born
        Sells microscope sets
1938 – Buys the American Flyer toy train company
1941 – Gilbert Hall of Science opens in New York City
1961 – Dies in New Haven, Connecticut
1967 – The A.C. Gilbert Company goes out of business
1989 – A.C. Gilbert's Discovery Village, a children's museum, opens in Salem, Oregon
1991 – The A.C. Gilbert Heritage Society forms for people to share their interest in A.C. Gilbert and the A.C. Gilbert Company

Author's Note

The incidents in this book are based on the writings of A.C. Gilbert. Some of the quotations are invented and included to aid the reader.

Bibliography

Bainbridge, John. "Profiles: American Boy." The New Yorker, December 20, 1952.

Gilbert, A.C. and McClintock, Marshall. The Man Who Lives In Paradise. New York: Rinehart and Company, 1954.

Heimburger, Donald J., ed. A.C. Gilbert's Heritage. River Forest, IL: Heimburger House Publishing Company, 1983.

Watson, Bruce. The Man Who Changed How Toys Are Made. New York: Viking, 2002.

Resources

A.C. Gilbert's Discovery Village – www.acgilbert.org

A.C. Gilbert Heritage Society – www.acghs.org

A.C. Gilbert Project – www.eliwhitney.org/gil/overview.htm

Bill Bean's Erector Set and A.C. Gilbert Website – www.erectorset.net

Erector World – www.girdersandgears.com

For Peggy Young – a magical mom

R.Y.

For Noah, Jonah, and Hannah – my inspiration

M.A.N.M.

Special thanks to: Uncle Jake Koehler for his gift of an Erector Set; Kim Baldwin, Pam Vorachek, Charlie Pack, and Bill Bean for sharing their A.C. expertise; Barry Lane for his good humor; Karen Antikajian for her editing eye; Mary Ann Nelson McAlister for creating reality out of a vision; and Ava Litton for her loving assistance on this long journey.

No part of this publication may be reproduced in whole or in part, or stored in a retrieval system, or transmitted in any for or by any means, electronically, mechanical, photocopying, recording, or otherwise without written permission from the copyright holder.

For permission contact Real Writing Press at realwriting@comcast.net

Copyright © 2011 by Real Writing Press
All rights reserved

ISBN 978-0-9742196-1-5

www.ingramcontent.com/pod-product-compliance
Lightning Source LLC
Chambersburg PA
CBRC092052040426
42446CB00006B/244